Perspectives
Disappearing Rainforests
What Are the Issues?

Series Consultant: Linda Hoyt

Flying Start
to Literacy®

Contents

Rainforests are being destroyed. Why does it matter?

Borneo is the third largest island in the world and the largest in Asia. Borneo is home to one of the oldest rainforests in the world. But the rainforests of Borneo are being cut down at an alarming rate to clear the land for farming and, in particular, for producing palm oil, which is in high demand worldwide.

What is the impact on people, animals and climate?

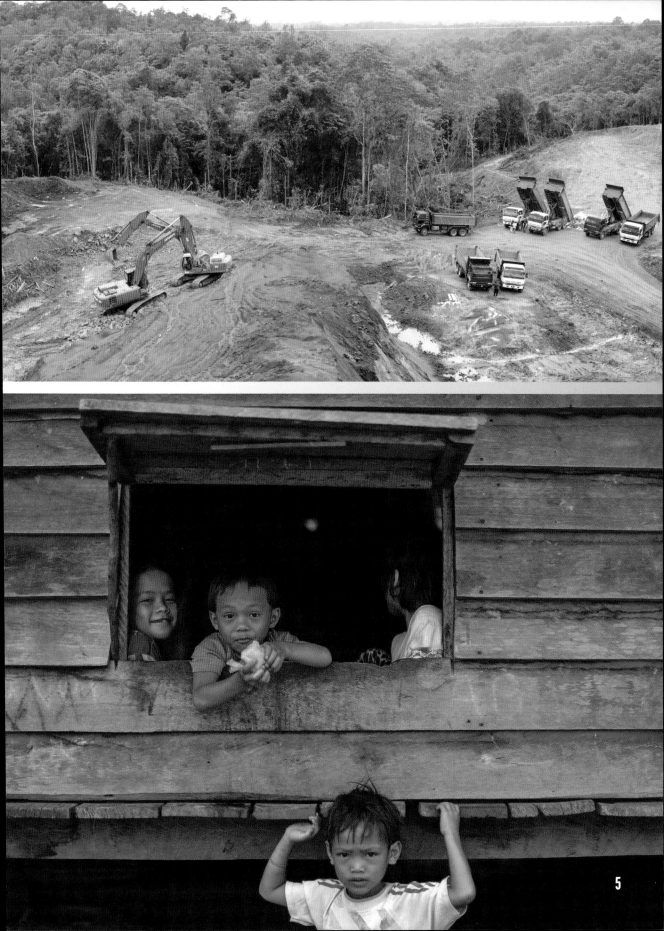

Orphans of the forest

Orphaned baby orangutans like Kedaung are a sad reminder of the dangers that confront orangutans when they lose their rainforest home. In this article, The Orangutan Project shares how far little Kedaung has come since he was rescued.

What is your response to the information in this article? Why do you feel this way?

Kedaung was estimated to be two years old when he was confiscated from a residence in North Sumatra in April 2013. He had numerous dog bite wounds on his body and was in a serious condition. Fighting for life, he was taken immediately to the Orangutan Quarantine Centre in North Sumatra where he was given intensive treatment and around-the-clock care.

Kedaung spent the next three years at the Quarantine Centre where he was given the highest quality care, food and vet treatment. He was socialised with other orangutans and became strong and inquisitive. In March 2016, he was transferred to an orangutan release site in preparation for release into the Sumatran jungle.

In this new environment, Kedaung has flourished. He enjoys playing and climbing in the socialisation cages, especially on the flexible rubber ropes. He also likes to play fight with other orangutans, rolling and play biting.

Kedaung is regularly taken out to "forest school" with his human caregivers. At five years of age, he is the youngest in forest school class but he is making great progress. When Kedaung was first taken to the forest he was hesitant to climb. However, he was coaxed with fruit placed in the trees by his caregivers to climb into the forest canopy. Recently, when he spent his first night in the forest with his school companion, Kedaung was observed making his own nest for the first time. This is one of the principal skills an orangutan must learn before being deemed ready to be released into the forest.

Unfortunately, there are many baby orangutans that aren't as lucky as Kedaung. Due to deforestation, many orangutans are left homeless and hungry and are an easy target for hunters. When these orangutans die, their babies become orphans. Many of these orphans die, too. Others are taken and sold to people who cannot care for them properly.

Orangutan rehabilitation centres are overcrowded due to this crisis. The Orangutan Project sends funds to support the care and rehabilitation of orphans like Kedaung. A huge focus is on habitat protection to ensure that these orphans will have a safe forest home to return to in the future.

Tribes struggle to survive in Borneo

This article is based on information from Survival International, a global group that fights for the rights of tribal people. It describes what is happening to the Penan people, so that the international community will be alerted to their situation.

Is it ethical to deprive the Penan people of their way of life?

The Penan tribe

The hunter-gatherer tribe, the Penan, live deep in the rainforests of Sarawak, a state in the Malaysian part of the island of Borneo. They are battling to stop the destruction of their last remaining forests and, with it, their way of life.

Their rights to the land they live on are not recognised by the Sarawak government, and their forests are being cleared for logging, oil palm plantations and hydroelectric dams, robbing them of their means of survival.

A long fight

The Penan have tried to stop their forest homes from being cut down. Over the past 40 years, they have set up many protests to stop the logging companies from entering their land. During one protest in 1987, they blockaded the roads that had been cut through the forest for logging trucks. More than one hundred Penan were arrested.

These protests have been unsuccessful. They have not stopped the logging. And once all the valuable trees are removed, large companies return and clear the remaining forest to set up oil palm plantations.

The Sarawak government also plans to build hydroelectric dams, which will flood the villages where the Penan live.

How do they live?

The rainforest provides the Penan with everything they need. They grow their own food. They use silent blowpipes and poison darts to hunt deer, wild pigs and other small animals. They also catch fish from the many rivers that run through their land. A member of the Penan tribe, Ba Lai, reinforced the importance of the rainforest to the Penan way of life:

> *We're not like the people in the towns, who have money and can buy things. If we lose all the things the forest gives us, we will die.*

In areas where the forests have been cleared for logging and oil palm plantations, it is becoming almost impossible for the Penan to sustain themselves.

Logging and oil palm

Cutting down the rainforest not only destroys the Penan's home – it also destroys the environment. When the forests are cut down, more soil and debris flow into the rivers when it rains. This kills the fish.

The number and size of the oil palm plantations that are established after the rainforest is cleared, means there is no land for the Penan.

Without their rainforest homes, many Penan are forced into poverty. They have to work on plantations and in small towns to earn money to buy the things they once grew and hunted.

If they lose their land completely, many Penan fear that they will no longer be independent – they will lose their culture.

Save orangutans!

The Orangutan Project was established in 1998 to ensure that endangered wild orangutan species would be protected against extinction. The organisation produced this poster to point out that orangutans are in danger because of the rapid growth of the palm oil industry. Is this poster effective? How does it persuade the reader?

THE BIG ORANGE ARMY

- Orangutans in Sumatra and Borneo are in grave danger. Every hour, 300 football grounds of precious remaining forest are cleared to make way for oil palm plantations.

- Palm oil is used in everything from snack foods to soaps. It is found in over half of all packaged items on our supermarket shelves.

- In the last 20 years, over 3.4 million hectares of Indonesian and Malaysian forests have been destroyed to make way for oil palm plantations.

- Almost 80% of orangutan habitat has disappeared in the last 20 years.

- We are losing over 6000 orangutans a year. We must stop this devastation in its tracks.

TAKE ACTION TODAY BEFORE IT'S TOO LATE

Rainforests in peril

In this article, Marcia Amidon Lusted explores the issue of deforestation.

Why are rainforests in peril? How could you make a difference?

Rainforests are not only one of the most amazing places on Earth, but they are also one of its most endangered environments. Why are the rainforests disappearing so quickly?

People can make money from harvesting the trees in the forest or using the land for other purposes. Huge trees, hundreds of years old, are cut down and sold as timber or burnt as firewood. To get logging trucks and equipment into these areas, more trees are cut down to build roads. Forests are cleared to make land for big and small farms to graze cattle. As the population of our planet grows, there are more people who need more land, and more rainforests are cut down to accommodate them.

Why is it a big deal if our planet loses its rainforests? There will be fewer plants and animals. Seventy per cent of the world's animals and plants live in rainforests. Many cannot survive without their forest homes.

And without the rainforest's trees, which help regulate the climate by cooling it and adding humidity, we will have hotter and drier weather. There will be fewer trees to absorb carbon dioxide and release it as oxygen for us to breathe. Burning timber to clear the rainforests also adds carbon dioxide to the atmosphere.

But what can we do to save the rainforests from disappearing? The conservation site mongabay.com says that it's as simple as:

TEACH others about how important the rainforests are.

RESTORE damaged ecosystems by replanting trees.

ENCOURAGE people to live in a way that doesn't hurt the environment.

ESTABLISH parks to protect the rainforests and their wildlife.

SUPPORT companies that minimise damage to the environment.

Palm oil puzzle:
The often untold story of a very amazing plant

This article quotes Denis J. Murphy who is Professor of Biotechnology at the University of South Wales in the United Kingdom. He is also an independent researcher and advisor to the Food and Agriculture Organization of the United Nations and the Malaysian Palm Oil Board.

How does Professor Murphy's information add to your understanding of the issues surrounding the production of palm oil?

The oil palm tree has been grown as a source of food by many people in western Africa for more than 4000 years. It has been, and still is, very important to people's health and well-being. Professor Denis J. Murphy says that people are ignorant about the value of palm oil. He states that there is another story about palm oil that is not well known, especially in richer countries.

No other crop can yield even half as much per hectare. In 2014, almost 70 million tonnes of palm oil were produced in the world. Over 85 per cent was used in food. If other crops were to replace palm oil in food, it would require at least 50 million additional hectares of farmland just to produce the same amount of edible oil that is currently produced on oil palm plantations.

This is the fruit from the oil palm tree. Palm oil is extracted from the fruit.

Why is this tree so unpopular? Today, Indonesia and Malaysia produce 85 per cent of the world's supply of palm oil. Rainforests are burnt down to clear land to grow oil palm plantations. As a result, native animals such as orangutans are being left homeless, as are indigenous people. Many people want to ban palm oil products ranging from cosmetics to chocolates.

Professor Murphy agrees there are many problems, but there are solutions. Cutting down native forest areas must eventually be stopped.

Palm oil is also a uniquely efficient edible crop that is essential for food security in Africa and Asia. Scientists, farmers, processors and consumers need to work together to develop solutions to the many problems that are faced by oil palm.

The problem with oil palm crops is where they are planted. So, instead of boycotting products containing palm oil, look for sustainable palm oil products. These products have been made without destroying any new protected rainforest areas. That way, you are doing your bit to protect the rainforests. And you are also helping the farmers that grow this remarkable crop.

In 2014, it is estimated that the world produced a massive 70 million tonnes of palm oil.

What is your opinion?: How to write a persuasive argument

1. State your opinion

Think about the issues related to your topic. What is your opinion?

2. Research

Research the information you need to support your opinion.

Related PERSPECTIVES book   Internet   Other sources

3. Make a plan

Introduction

How will you "hook" the reader?

State your opinion.

List reasons to support your opinion.

What persuasive devices will you use?

Reason 1
Support your reason
with evidence and details.

Reason 2
Support your reason
with evidence and details.

Reason 3
Support your reason
with evidence and details.

Conclusion

Restate your opinion. Leave your reader with a strong message.

4. Publish

Publish your persuasive argument.

Use visuals to reinforce your opinion.